My World of Geography

RIVERS

Angela Royston

Heinemann Library
Chicago, Illinois

© 2005 Heinemann Library
a division of Reed Elsevier Inc.
Chicago, Illinois

Customer Service 888-454-2279
Visit our website at www.heinemannlibrary.com

Design: Ron Kamen and Celia Jones
Illustrations: Jo Brooker (p. 11), Jeff Edwards
  (pp. 5, 28–29)
Photo Research: Rebecca Sodergren, Melissa Allison, and
  Debra Weatherley
Originated by Ambassador Litho
Printed and bound in China by South
China Printing

09 08 07
10 9 8 7 6 5 4 3 2

Library of Congress
Cataloging-in-Publication Data
Royston, Angela.
  Rivers / Angela Royston.
    p. cm. – (My world of geography)
  Includes bibliographical references and index.
  ISBN 1-4034-5594-5 (HC), 1-4034-5603-8 (Pbk)
  ISBN 978-1-4034-5594-9 (HC), 978-1-4034-560
  3-8 (Pbk)
  1. Rivers–Juvenile literature. I. Title. II. Series.
  GB1203.8.R69 2005
  551.48'3–dc22
                              200400387

Acknowledgments
The author and publisher are grateful to the following for permission to reproduce copyright material:
pp. 4 (Jacques Jangouse), 9 (Robert Harding Picture Library/T. Gervis), 24 (Adrian Arbib) Alamy Images; p. 6 (Caron Phillipe) Corbis Sygma; pp. 7 (George Huey), 14 (Yann Arthus-Bertrand), 16 (Eye Ubiquitous/J. Waterlow), 19 (Kevin Schafer), 20 (Roman Soumar), 21 (Charles O'Rear), 22 (Yann Arthus-Bertrand), 23 Corbis; p. 8 (David Williams) Photo Library Wales; p. 10 London Aerial Photo Library; pp. 12 (Martin Bond), 17 (Robert Brook) Science Photo Library; p. 13 (Pavel Rahman) Associated Press; p. 15 Harcourt Education Ltd.; pp. 18, 26, 27 Getty Images/Photodisc; p. 25 Geoscience Features.

Cover photograph reproduced with permission of Getty Images/Stone.

Contents

Some words are shown in bold, **like this.** You can find out what they mean by looking in the glossary.

What Is a River?

A river is a large stream of water that flows across the land. It usually starts high on a mountain. It ends when it flows into the sea or a lake.

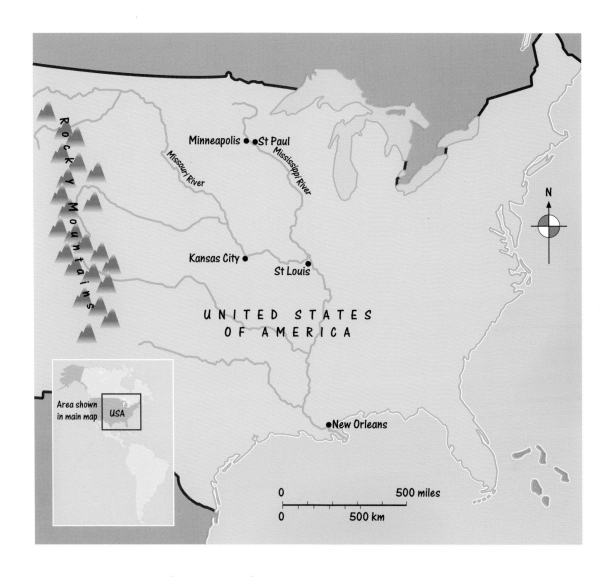

This map shows the rivers as wiggly blue lines. Rivers are always colored blue on maps, even if they look brown in real life.

Where Do Rivers Begin?

The **source** of a river is the place where it begins. Sometimes water flows from a hole in the ground called a **spring.** The springwater might even be hot!

The water in this hot spring sprays up from deep inside Earth.

Water runs down a hill or mountain
when it rains or when snow melts. The
flowing water forms many tiny streams.
Some streams join together to make a
bigger stream.

River Valleys

A stream flows down a hill or mountain to the **valley** below. As it flows along, it is joined by other streams. Soon the stream becomes a river.

Rivers wash away stones and soil as they flow along. Sometimes a river slowly wears away rock to make a deep valley or **canyon.**

It took millions of years for the Colorado River to make the Grand Canyon in Arizona.

Flowing Over Flat Land

The river then leaves the mountains and flows over flatter land. It becomes wider and the water flows more slowly. Sometimes a river flows around higher land and forms a large bend.

This river flows through the city of Durham in the United Kingdom.

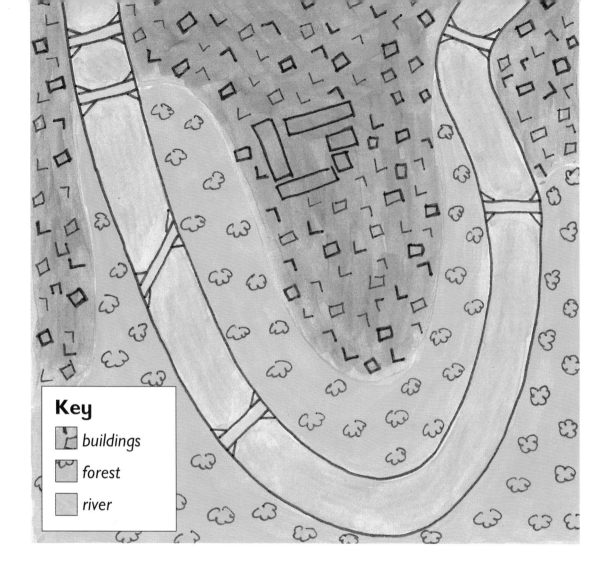

Key

🏢 buildings

🌳 forest

▨ river

This map shows the same stretch of
river as in the photograph. You can
see how the river bends and where
the bridges cross the river. You could
draw a map like this.

Flooding

When snow melts in the mountains, more water flows into rivers. Rivers may become so full they **overflow.** Rivers also may overflow if it rains a lot.

Sometimes the water gets higher than the **banks** of the river and flows into the land nearby. If there is a town or city near the river, the water may **flood** the streets.

Reaching the Sea

The **mouth** of a river is where the river flows into the sea. There, fresh river water mixes with salty seawater.

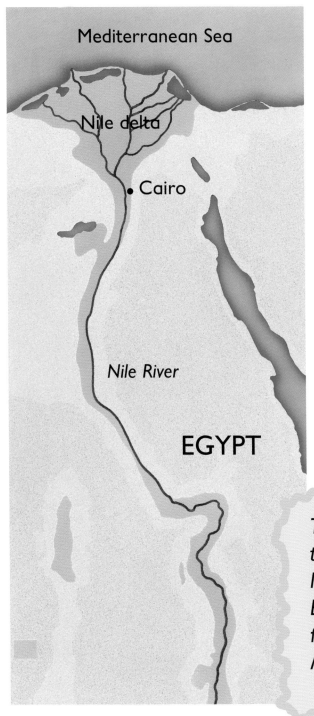

Mediterranean Sea

Nile delta

• Cairo

Nile River

EGYPT

A river is widest at its mouth. Sometimes the river mouth spreads out to make a triangle shape called a **delta. Banks** of mud form in the river's mouth.

This map shows the delta of the Nile River in Egypt. The Nile flows into the Mediterranean Sea.

Using River Water

Farmers may use river water to water the fields nearby. They dig ditches or use pipes to take the water from the river to the fields.

People use river water in **factories** and in homes. **Paper mills** use a lot of water. They are often built on the **banks** of a river.

Traveling by River

People use boats to travel along rivers. The boats take them from one town to another. In some countries, it is easier to travel by river than by road!

This boat is taking people on a river trip.

Where there is no bridge, people can
use a boat or a **ferry** to cross the
river. Ferries can carry people, cars,
trucks, or farm animals.

Carrying Goods

Riverboats carry things, as well as people. In some places, farmers carry fruits and vegetables by boat to sell in the towns and cities.

These women are selling fruits and vegetables at a floating market in Thailand.

Trees are often taken down rivers to be made into **timber** and paper. The logs are pushed into the water and floated **downstream.** They do not need to be put on a boat.

Ports

Ports are towns where ships load and unload **goods.** Ships carry goods across the sea. Many ports are at the **mouths** of rivers.

The port of Manaus in Brazil is hundreds of miles up the Amazon River.

Some ports are a long way up the river. Big ships can sail far in deep, wide rivers. Smaller boats take goods to ports in narrow or **shallow** rivers.

Rivers in Danger

Rivers are easily harmed. If people take too much water from a river, the river may dry up.

Many **factories** pour **waste chemicals** into rivers. Chemicals that farmers put on their fields get into rivers, too. Some of these chemicals poison the water and kill the fish.

Enjoying Rivers

Many people go to rivers for fun. Paddling a **kayak** through fast-flowing water is very exciting. Some slow, gentle rivers are good places to swim, but only if the water is clean.

Many people enjoy a quiet walk along the **banks** of a river. Fishing can be fun, too. But it can be difficult to catch a fish in water that is moving quickly.

Rivers of the World

This map shows some of the biggest and longest rivers in the world.

Mackenzie

NORTH AMERICA

Missouri

St Lawrence

Colorado

Mississippi

Rio Grande

Amazon

SOUTH AMERICA

Mississippi-Missouri
Key fact: The Mississippi-Missouri is the longest river in North America.
Length: 3,740 miles (6,019 km)

Amazon
Key fact: The Amazon is the second longest river in the world.
Length: 4,000 miles (6,437 km)

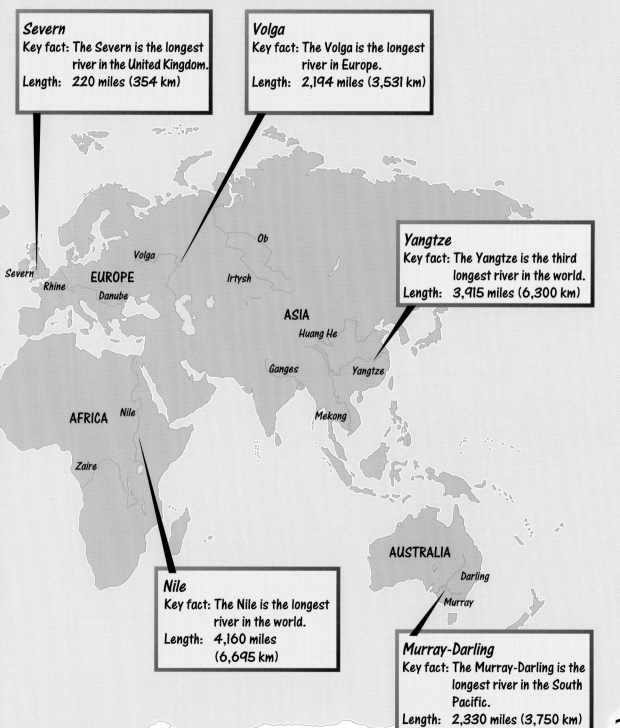

Severn
Key fact: The Severn is the longest river in the United Kingdom.
Length: 220 miles (354 km)

Volga
Key fact: The Volga is the longest river in Europe.
Length: 2,194 miles (3,531 km)

Yangtze
Key fact: The Yangtze is the third longest river in the world.
Length: 3,915 miles (6,300 km)

Nile
Key fact: The Nile is the longest river in the world.
Length: 4,160 miles (6,695 km)

Murray-Darling
Key fact: The Murray-Darling is the longest river in the South Pacific.
Length: 2,330 miles (3,750 km)

Severn

Rhine

EUROPE

Danube

Volga

Ob

Irtysh

ASIA

Huang He

Ganges

Yangtze

Mekong

Nile

AFRICA

Zaire

AUSTRALIA

Darling

Murray

ANTARCTICA

Glossary

bank land along the edge of a river

canyon narrow valley with steep cliffs on each side

chemicals substances used by farmers and in factories

delta river mouth in the shape of a triangle

downstream downhill direction that a river flows

factory place where people make things

ferry boat used to carry people, cars, and other things

flood fill with water

goods things that are made, bought, and sold

kayak narrow boat that you move along using a paddle

mouth where a river meets the sea

overflow spill over

paper mill factory that makes paper

port town or city where ships load and unload

shallow not deep

source place where a river or stream begins

spring place where a stream of water bubbles up out of the ground

timber lengths of wood cut from tree trunks

valley low land between two or more hills or mountains

waste leftover materials that people do not want

More Books to Read

Ashwell, Miranda, and Andy Owen. *Rivers.* Chicago: Heinemann Library, 1998.

Chambers, Catherine. *Flood.* Chicago: Heinemann Library, 2002.

Galko, Francine. *River Animals.* Chicago: Heinemann Library, 2003.

Giesecke, Ernestine. *River Plants.* Chicago: Heinemann Library, 1999.

Hewitt, Sally. *Rivers, Ponds, and Seashore.* New York: Millbrook Press, 1999.

Klingel, Cynthia Fitterer, and Robert B. Noyed. *The Mississippi River.* Chanhassen, Minn.: Child's World, 2000.

Morris, Neil. *Earth's Changing Rivers.* Chicago: Raintree, 2003.

Winne, Joanne. *Living Near a River.* Danbury, Conn.: Scholastic Library, 2000.

Index